WATER DAMAGE

Other Books by the Author

At the Gates of the Theme Park (Mansfield Press, 2010)
Wild Clover Honey and the Beehive: 28 Sonnets on the Sonnet (with Stephen Brockwell; Rideau River Press, 2004)
The Shape Inside: 12 Sonnets (New Formalist ebooks, 2003)
After Stillness (above/ground press, 2003)

WATER DAMAGE

PETER NORMAN

for Roger —

with best wishes,

MANSFIELD PRESS

a stuart ross book

Printed in Canada

Library and Archives Canada Cataloguing in Publication

Norman, Peter, 1973-
Water damage / Peter Norman.

Poems.
ISBN 978-1-77126-008-4

I. Title.

PS8627.O76W38 2013 C811'.6 C2013-901253-2

Editor for the Press: Stuart Ross
Cover Design: Denis De Klerck
Cover Image: Shutterstock
Typesetting: Stuart Ross
Author Photo: Melanie Little

The publication of *Water Damage* has been generously supported by the Canada Council for the Arts and the Ontario Arts Council.

Mansfield Press Inc.
25 Mansfield Avenue, Toronto, Ontario, Canada M6J 2A9
Publisher: Denis De Klerck
www.mansfieldpress.net

to the memory of John Lavery

CONTENTS

UP NEAR WAWA

Up near Wawa, where the 17
was lightning-lit and slicked
with flagellating rain and hit
repeatedly with hailstones;
up near Wawa, weary
of the pummelled 17, we saw a buck
self-mortify on an advancing rig.
I say self-mortify, which is to say
in fact it ran, confused or mad,
straight for the grille, the brights, but like
atoners and their sniping whips perhaps
it thought the sins of herbivores,
or just its own, or those of every deer,
might gather in its blood and dissipate,
run guttered on the gleaming grate,
spatter on the road and disappear.

But wait.
I got it wrong.
There never was a buck.
Or moose. No elk, no lowly mole.
The rain was real as hooves for sure and kept
the frantic wipers set on highest whine
and lightning really lit the way
with winking glimpses of the broken line.
Up near Wawa, yes, the 17,
and rigs for sure, their bright relentless chain,
and yes, there was this one oncoming truck
with high beams, nearly croaked us in the rain.
The rest, I guess, is wrong. There was no buck.

WHAT I MEANT

I think I forgot to set the switch to OFF.
I fear I may have let somebody down.
Hear that? The grinding of teeth in the wall?

Amid the sibilance of furnaces
and air-con units, when we tangled legs
and trembled: was that tenderness?

Who mans the door and checks the ticket stubs
and stamps the hands? I dearly hope—
I mean this, now—I haven't let you down.

The fan jammed or the alternator blew
or something slipped its joint.
They did what they could but

what can you do? Please keep me
from the mounted sheet of glass
and any light that bounces off that glass.

I'll row you across to the opposite shore,
which is verdant. We'll sit there. We'll eat.
We'll do it tomorrow, I promise. Maybe next week.

DRIED MY EYES

Dried my eyes
and slunk out of the tower where I worked
and found the smokers clustered by the door,
coughing, shooting shit, recounting
how one day the big red bell
struck itself, repeatedly,
because of smoke.

Having dried my eyes, I spotted
all the paper blowing down the street.
The articles and photographs and letters to an editor
who never answered. All the adult classifieds.

My eyes would not stay dry.
In bars I couldn't see the TV sets.
Could not make out the score.
Could not discern the urgent headline
scrolling underneath a shot of coifs
and mouths ajar to let opinions out.
I couldn't see the latest, and I wept.

I'm in good company. Don't mock.
Da Vinci wept. The Brontë sisters wept.
Marcel Marceau evinced that he was weeping.
Every major prophet must have wept—
the things they would have seen!
And monsters wept. Yes, Himmler wept
and Torquemada in his toils wept.

Surgeons worked my moistened eye,
stripped out the blots
that hovered everywhere I peered.
Efficient as a dagger's tip
they went too far, too deep,
and scoured my sight.

Printed words have blurred into a cipher.
Cloudy symbols and their high romance
are hieroglyphic now. My fingers itch
for Braille prowess, but that's a long way off—
the classes don't resume until next year.

Somewhere beyond the old screen door
that's meant to keep mosquitoes out
but fails because it's gashed,
figures lurch and stumble from the marsh.
I cannot see them come.

You listening, Doc?
Yeah, you who wrecked my eyes?
You hear the slurp as legs work free
from gripping muck? You hear the bulrush break?
Mistakes don't disappear. Their discharge festers.

TRACTS

Someone puts tracts in my mailbox. They come disguised as coupons. Eager for deals on veggies or shampoo, I open them. They say I'm headed for Hell. They list the punishments I can expect when I arrive. These are severe, to say the least, and apparently go on forever, without even a short break. The tracts point out that if I had repented my sins to Christ, I would have been saved. Too late now, they explain. It is foretold that a precise number of souls will get into Heaven, but the number was reached long ago.

I would like the tracts to stop. I watch my mailbox all day. No one comes. And yet when I peek in, it's there: another tract. It tells me I can't avoid what's due. My wickedness demands that I be judged. I look around. Up and down the street, my gaze takes a stroll. Willow trees kneel to pray. Stout shrubs tilt in supplication. Fervour grips the street, and penitence, and pleas that we be saved, all of us, even the shrubs. Well, either that or the wind's picked up. You'd be amazed how the wind can make stuff bend.

TRIPTYCH

Have we not donned helmets with built-in lamps?
Haven't we traversed a sloping floor

and air got scarce and stalagmites
grew taller as we trod?

Didn't we have chisels and shovels and picks,
and batter in fever to get to the base

of all things? Finding a lake,
did we not slip in and swim

as deep as our lungs would allow?
How to plumb the ultimate ground,

break through to a ceiling of stars?

*

Weather today was a mongrel.
The snow came in handfuls of shot.

Hard little fuckers, half hail,
the heads of the smallest of nails.

Then sunshine. Then clouds in swift convoy
to some cloud crisis over the lake—

and they broke. Peering from under
a tattered umbrella, my neighbour

pointed right up. *It's madness.*
I nodded and answered, *It's mad.*

Is there something you'd rather I'd said?

*

Doctors forbid me to deep-sea dive.
Dabbling in a backyard pool,

I busted the skin of a lung. At ER
they primed the sternal saw

to pry the ribs like Lamborghini doors—
a plan that I'm glad to report was aborted.

My sternum's intact, and my cure
was pure nature, the workings of time.

I'll tell you straight: the creek's not deep
but nor have I clogged it with mud.

You're free to examine the bed.

FRIDAY AFTERNOON

Someone taught the stutterer to utter lines with rich mellifluence.
I've a tough time pushing such sluggish syllables out.
Domineer me, stir the old churn, and my mouth reverts molasses-ward.
All of which is fine should suaveness in its finery be disowned.
Still the fingertip thrills to silk. The monarch's vestment bristles with invisible
threads. They must be not seen to be believed. They dazzle on a Friday
when the factory siren whines day's end. We all spill out, pop beers
and gape. Some call bull, but never me. I want to be seduced.

The beer is froth. My shift broke all my nails.
The royal carriage wears a crust of mould.
I'm dusting off an old silk robe too fine for eyes.
I can't quite get a sentence out—I'd make a lousy judge.
Someone tore the light out of my clothes. Someone set alight
the tar behind my slick, bruised lips
and the consonants' fat legs are getting mired.

ON THE OCCASION OF HER MAJESTY'S PASSING MY HOUSE IN A BOAT

O Queen, you are passing my house.
O Queen, you are perched upon a giant boat.
O Queen, big boats line up to honour you.
Sailors doff their caps and cheer.

Queen, you are dressed in white.
Queen, you look so classy.
Queen, I guess you define classy, though, so,
Queen, I'm sorry I misspoke.

O Queen, you have passed my house.
O Queen, from my wooden deck I waved.
Queen, I doubt you saw me.
I was far, far away and appeared very tiny.

Dartmouth, Nova Scotia, 2010

PLEA

Open the door. My knuckle's raw from knocking.
Come on, I need your bandages
and salves. I need the mired fly.

You've mentioned that we tend to have the same
damn conversation every time. You're right.
I'll think of something new to say. I'll shock you.

Unlock the lock. The deadbolt's asinine.
You're better than this stubbornness. At heart
you're warm and pliable. Undo the chain.

I only came around because of these—
my knuckles, daubed with pus.
Don't worry how they got that way.

Unseal the skylight. Free the basement hatch
and let it swing and disappear
into its hutch of shade.

We have so much to talk about, to plan.
I brought a roll of bandages to share.
Beneath my ribs—you feel?—the flies are hatching.

FROM WISDOM OF THE ROCK, BOOK IV

Okay, I may be igneous
but not so igneous as you imagine,
ignoramus.

I like to think that I am stratified.
That I am sedimentary.
That fossils at my root betray

the primal urge. I have endured
for plenty of millennia, right here,
here at the foothill's base.

I have acquired. I have absorbed.
A certain wisdom seeped into my bulk.
Igneous or not, I suffer too.

THE ANSWERS

How do you quantify what has not happened?

That's not really a story you'd want to print.

My colleagues in the physiology department
didn't know what I was doing—
if they had, they might have made trouble.

I spent a lot of time, well,
entertaining
goodness knows how many
dignitaries—a lot of
shall we say
senior executives.

Peter, if you were charged
with the task of calling these same guys
I did, and they didn't know you
from a bale of hay,
you may have got a different response.

I don't think their background speaks well of them.

You wouldn't think of him
as being a skier;
he didn't have any teeth.

This is quite a long saga.

All along we've been told
no, no, no,
everything's going ahead as planned
over and over and over again.

SCHOOL DAY

Umber lights and guards' batons
indicate the influx of us krill
schlepping satchels, bending cowled
against the hemophilic sleet.
Chain-link scars abut the street.
They tore, years past, had ins and outs
for us to enter or escape,
which since are sutured up.

One gap survives. The duty minotaur
totes a clipboard, notches one by one
our comings in. His pen's gone sick with starch.
By the bike racks, downing milt, subsist
the pupae that were gutted, gelded, stomped—
schooled, we call it—when the bell began to toll.

UNDERPASS

Some crew was here.
The Class of '17 was here.
Brandon who reportedly sucks cock was here.
The person with the number 222-9198 was here.

Bottles were here but were shattered.
Rigs with syringes full.
Prophylactics in their packages
and clean, untarnished cigarettes.

I killed and ate a meal here,
carved a mission statement,
plucked a haggard tune.
I lost what husk was left of what I cared about, right here.

All the voices of the Earth are funnelled here.
They speak into my open ear.
I hope that you will join me here
and lie with me upon a gravel bed.

A poorly rendered penis was right here.
A name of great illegibility.
A promise of unceasing love.
The blind will see, the crippled walk. We're waiting, here.

LIFE IS UNFAIR

In the days I was allotted,
coins of all denominations
dropped out of my pockets.

Penny, nickel, quarter, buck—
years amassed; a modest fortune
simply fell away.

Yet in those years I walked through rain
and hail. I courted lightning.
Skies got troubles off their chests and onto me.

Throughout those years, my pockets loitered
on my pants, mouths open to the air—
and not a single coin has fallen in.

EIGHT KISSES

A man holds an apple to his lips. He kisses it.
Another man, the lover of the first,
touches his own lips
to that same skin.

Across the street, a woman in her yard
pecks an apple that she grew and picked.
Her son's off smooching
with another apple altogether.

The son has a friend in a far-off town
who frenches with a far-off apple there.
Her twin tongues yet another—
licks its literal core!

Their father (who abandoned them
and makes his living now
on a frigate that patrols the mid-Pacific)
osculates a rotted apple in his bunk.

The captain smacks
an apple of his own, which is rot-free.
He gives it a playful bite
the night before the mutiny.

All of which is just to say
many muscles are needed for a kiss.
Also to bite and to chew. And you,
I felt, of everyone I know, would like to know of this.

EVEN

Even the last crushed can
fetched from the deeps of the fat blue bin
in which we keep the empty things
lives in hope as the old man's hand
drops it in a reeking plastic
hamper filled with other cans
that there in the stench of the depot
to which it knows it's headed
where it will be flung on appropriate heaps
and carted away and reduced
into a single useful element
a moment might occur
where some grand shudder
ripples through the depot's
mounds and bundles,
makes them shift in unison
and so impels them to believe
that when the whole procedure is complete
and all of them are mere, pure
plastic, metal, glass or pulp,
their differences will burn away,
the categories will dissolve
and all this motley mess of outcast crap
will thus emerge the other end
clean and buffed
and functional
and one

(though cans
don't think that much
and are not metaphysically inclined
and being crushed might dampen
daydreams of such scope—
the can's got plenty else to fret about)

(and yet, old friend,
who drank with me
the contents of that can,
who slurred your words recounting
criminal adventures of our youth,
will you deny there's comfort
in pretending this aluminum
accordion can hope, 'cause after all,
if it can do so, even now,
what excuse is there for us,
for you and me,
to wallow in a marsh of anecdote
and count our missing hairs and swear
the future is the candle brimmed and gagging
on a pool of its own body
processed into something new
and worse?).

THE TURNIPS

after bpNichol

The turnips ooze a juice just visible on his chin.
Etiquette-bereft, the cad inturps the conversation I was in.
In the urn's pit, ash accumulates: mortality's pith.
A tin spur goads moans from the lover I lie with.
Poking the proxy doll with a rustpin makes for anguish.
Don't stunrip the ne'er-do-wells. Just let 'em languish.
Pit urns fill with spit-out pits of fruit.
Baffling ritpuns offend the ruling brute.
Punstir the ticklish for a ribald effect.
A nut rips when the razor swipes. Your denim won't protect.
On the suntrip, bronzed-up tourists tipple plonk.
Untrips are offered. The unship's waiting at the dock.
Writhe and spin, rut and grunt among the scented sheets.
Runspit in thickets like a rabid boar in heat.
Pitnurs leave me stumped. From a small stump I orate.
Runt, sip that rancid wine. You'll find it tastes of acetate.
Bail out the punt, sir, or the ferried souls will drown.
Your turn: sip the sugared venom, force it down.
The tip runs off on tipsy legs, leaving the servers broke.
Turps in turpish venues tell the filthiest of jokes.
        Spurtin' depravity, he mounted the stump—and spoke—

MAN WITH DAISY

She loves me for my soothing voice
and silken touch.

Loves me not
because I have bad teeth.

She loves me when I brandish dental tools,
loves me not when cracking jokes I go too far
and say the only thing
you never say.

She loves me for I sing to her
and by my singing butterflies are lured.

She loves me not.
There's nothing here to love.
I'm just a wreck of egg and sperm.
Other one-celled creatures swimming by
said, *God, I'm glad it wasn't me.*

She loves me for the tenderness
behind the razor trick
but not the trick itself.

Loves me for my missing ear
not for the bloodied box.

IN THE CLINIC

The doctor measures pulse with a finger on the wrist.
The nurse prefers a band that grips the bicep.
The doctor utters numbers as the pulse count mounts.
Her finger is cool as perpetual shade.
Reading a meter, the nurse tells her figure.
Ending the tally, the doctor murmurs hers.
The nurse's slacks are purple and synthetic.
The doc has an appendix in a jar.

I have a query to put to the doctor.
I've got an urgent question for the nurse.
The unloved organ culled by the doctor
sulks in its brine. As for the nurse,
the purple of her slacks has breached the air,
a sopping bandage, a ballooning scar.

DR. F ATTENDS A SHOW

after Margaret Atwood

i

Watch close: there's a quick, distinct tic the performer
is prone to. Did you see? There? As the jewels glittered
and the dress shimmered in stage moonlight, she bent
a wrist with awkward zest; her eye focused
right offstage, into that emptiness
where pulleys lurk, and cast-off clothes. No lights, no cheers,
just the glint of a prop scalpel.

ii

Her lazy eye, when the wrist flicks, finds the offstage void,
the silence it hankers to behold.
A glimpse of that grave space accompanies the twist
of the wrist—a tic that sends the bad eye off
away from the clamour of the living,
from us and our palm-slapping love. Good thing we're not in the round.
Good thing, she thinks, the audience doesn't close behind me,
leaving me exposed as a sheared pomegranate,
marooned on a pad of hot stage light.

iii

Back in the lab, a patient's on a slab. Shy to confront
the fact the patient's passed from breathing soul to lifeless thing,
you left it on the slab in case it moves,
in case its waist should give a sudden thrust,
in case when rope constrains a straining arm the arm fights back,
in case the hand in its constraint finds life and claws
its shreds of rope. In case a heave of blood

sends it spilling from the cut
you made with less than diligent precision,
believing then the body was like other specimens
on other slabs. That's back in the lab. Applaud
for now the show, the star. Forget the lab, its harsh white lights, the cat
that rubs along the tables' legs. Anatomized
but still one piece, the patient stirs. The patient has a deep and secret
love, or maybe rage, for his anatomizer. You.

iv

This is no time to think of the lab, of you.
Diversion's what you need. But like
your patient, you have shackles at your ankles,
the dun scar of a branding at your navel.
Joints of you were finished by the weaver
of thick black stitch. Ten donors gave your fingers.
Doctor, none's more composite than you!
Nor more composed. You're steely as the ropes
and webs of net that hold your organs in
and keep their insurrections down.
Rise now! It's an ovation! Its thunder fills the shell-
shaped hall. The patchwork plating of your skull
is hidden by your pilfered flesh, and you
regard the blazing stage with borrowed eyes.

v

Doctor, we're admirers of your skill.
We magnify your artistry, for it is perfect.
Faced with rot's affront, we choose instead
submission to your work. The tiny seed
that you implant (the brief pinch makes us wince)
will burrow, fester, blossom with results

worth every polished cent. There between
essence and shadow lives your craft. Rotten
drapes are blown aside. Time's defied. Your presence
buckles our knees. We praise you as a god.
We in the surrounding seats, we have tendons
gone slack, knuckles puckered, weary aches in our sinews.
We've served our turn. We are but shafts of mines
too long plundered. So we turn to you.
You shine with kind intent, with Lazarus potential.
We beam. We grip your hand, ignore the smell.

vi

Lazarus lay there, larval,
awaiting that long-ago proxy for you,
writhing to life in his silken covering,
squirming as rot was repealed in his skin.
The tale is preached and the Good Book read
but we know the facts are distorted.
When Lazarus strode forth, starved,
cobweb-groggy, he encountered you.
Around him were the stunned, the converts, running
in fear and awe through veils of rain.
But he looked you in the eye with his withered eye. He demanded a motive.
He extended a long, fleshless finger and unmasked you.

vii

The room thickens with ovation. The show has stolen
every pretence of resistance. Oh, how we needed
release! We clap and weep. We've lost the ability
not to adore. We cry with hope that we need never suffer
any further. Might our selves entire be transmuted,
rendered incorruptible? Doctor, I am
desperate it be so. My chest is tender, my head is numb.
Back in the lab, the patient's awake, brain sopping with murder.

Eyes roll, waiting for the spark to make them see.
Breathe easy: those mismatched orbs are still incapable.
I have only adulation for you, sir. No murder in my brain.
I love you, crave you, as do all these good people.

viii

Rumours are getting wise. It's whispered you dared
attempt in your youth full messianic wonders.
There are certain glories man must not pursue.
In secret, though, we hope your plea won't be denied
and all your brilliance can light our gutted mines.
Whispers crackle like hearth logs in winter.
Whispers rasp in our skulls like the sea in the shell
and wrap us with wool in the cold.
Whispers ease our gravest pain.
Some of us heed the messages.
Most of us know such rumours are not solid,
only hopeful sighs—vain, the heart's
Morse pleading. Wishbones, we admit, are merely dregs of food.

ix

As we gather coats from our seats, a monster
raises from its slab a badly cobbled head,
jabs fingers into tall electric
sentries that you built to guard the place.
The monster moves like a slab of ice
sliding on the mat of its own melting. On timid feet,
one furred, one smooth, he edges through sporadic fires
set by toppled machines. Ambulation! Happiness!
The glee of a thing that can motor itself!
Fires drive him out to the moon's fainter light.
He reaches long arms toward it,
stalks it like an ill-trained hunter
unschooled in stealth. Light paints patterns
on the skin of his brow, which is leather.

x

We bustle into the cold, donning hats, coats, the hackle
of a boa. The moon spreads
insinuation on the ceiling,
reaches its rays for all horizons,
swells in its advance like a snowball.
We gossip and chitter. Everyone says
the performance was pure splendour. A shadow
moves at our fringes. Doctor, when you prepared the table
(the slab), secured the last length of leash,
what halted you mid-bind: a longing
for this very escape? For this gnashing of multi-hued teeth?
A cataclysmic howl and he is loose
among us. Can you fathom what it was
that flipped your will, compelled the knife
to slice the bonds? How will you heal
our mauled mouths, the new holes in our sides,
the bellies slit from chin to crotch? You won't. With him you'll prowl
for newer kills. The oaths are dead. You heed a keener call.

MAROONED

We watched a jellyfish pulled in to land,
flexing in vain against the tide:
a spectral sac with livid guts inside
and tentacles that dragged along the sand.
The ocean won. The jellyfish was hauled
onto a bed of rock. Congealing there
under the suffocating weight of air,
it sagged. The guts went dim. I was appalled,
but you suggested we should leave it be.
The kids were swimming; tentacles could raise
a mighty welt. Besides, you said, it pays
to let the sea administer the sea.

We did. The kids were fine. The tide withdrew,
marooning us with all its residue.

SABBATH SHIFT

Last Sabbath I scurried
over seaside rock
as ocean rose to break itself
against the lighthouse wall.

The sun was present only
as a pale wafer pressed
into the waiting flesh
of a congregant's hand.

Conifer curtains assaulted me.
Venom did its Trojan trick
by hiding in the rain.
Slowly my clothes corroded.

In a cottage cockeyed
on its hilltop squalled
a wet quartet of infants born
that morning to a halfwit,

waiting for me, my fingers,
nimble and able, to dart
into throats, clearing passage
through mucus for air.

Much work ahead,
and this a Sabbath.
Disdain, I knew, sat prim
in the vestry chairs.

But on I sprinted, duty's vassal.
How they squirmed and whined,
the infants I would save,
the priests on wooden seats.

Through mist and trees
and heaving surf
their voices chewed my heels,
licked my mossy toes.

I'm sure you know the pattern here.
The poison water falling.
Elders' rage and newborn pain,
and through the chaos, someone softly calling...

EVERYTHING ARISES FROM THE SOUND

Everything arises from the sound.
Town glows across a gap
of darkness, which is water.
The moon rose red but then regained its pallor.

Town is a garden of lights whose roots
tangle unseen in the sound.
Nothing's moving on the sound
except reflected lights, their trickery.

No boats are on the water anymore.
One came near, but then it ran aground.
Shoals are cruel and hulls are frail.
What doesn't sink arises from the sound.

IN PRAISE OF THE TOP THREE CELLPHONE MANUFACTURERS, AS DETERMINED BY GLOBAL MARKET SHARE IN 2010

O Nokia. Noblest of providers, number one
by far in market share. Nokia,
Finnish firm located in Espoo,
your Siemens network seminal.
Nabob nodular, Nokia!

Samsung, Samsung, second place
in market share. Samsung, munificent
and based in buzzing Seoul. O juggernaut
of gadgetry, purveyor of true pulse,
sung is your glory, sung is your praise.

O LG, spawn of Koo In-Hwoi,
titan too of Seoul, indeed
life's good. LG, your logarithm rings
and we consumers cry: *LG, LG, LG.*
In market share you're number three.

NEIGHBOURHOOD SONGS

i. The neighbour's music rumbles in the walls

I've had so many angel figurines. Bought them, housed them, stood them on my shelves in glorious array. I've fluffed their wings (at least those wings that were of feathers, hair or other stuff that can be teased by hand) and straightened up their halos. Chubby girls with rosy spots on pallid cheeks; lean, forceful Michaels with their trumpets thrust aloft; the flounciest of toddlers toting harps of brass. Whole cabinets have been devoted. They've conquered closets, populated tabletops. They've copulated in organics bins; cherubic offspring roil among the maggots that subsist on rotten sop. They skate along the ceiling, loiter on the floor. Inside the pipe that lurks inside the wall, their shadows gather, waiting for the day the drain's unstopped.

ii. Construction cranes make shadows on my yard

Some fellow pounded at my door. I thought he was soliciting, but no: he said he was a fugitive. No need to be alarmed. He only asked a place to stay, a fridge to pilfer from, a host that he could terrorize and bind. I acquiesced. What can I say? It does get lonesome here among the figurines, the cats and fur, the mounds of dust that whisper in the corner—busybodies, whispering of me. Bring on the tattooed thug, the con with heat packed in his briefs, the drooling perp—such company can tempt, at certain times. I let him in; he struck my chin and clenched my throat and tenderized my belly. Using twine I keep to guide my houseplants' growth he tied me up. He mouthed the words of songs by famous crooners, sighed the verse of poets we have read in gilded books. His teeth were green or maybe grey. He spoke of spiders that resided in his throat. His brow was crowned with sweat.

iii. It's potluck time and I can barely cook

Who thinks she's free is not. Who thinks he's wise is mummified in bandage lengths of dumb. Who clarions that we're community, yet stole my gnomes and tagged my backyard shed, is hypocrite incarnate. No one sees the dreadful things my neighbours do to me. And then the stranger comes, the devil guised as angel figurine, binding me with twine and winches and nobody stirs. Nobody comes to call. Nobody bears obligatory turnips from their yard, or greeting cards, or liquor mickeys 'cause I fed their pet or held their mail when they were gone. Bahamian palm trees shaded them; sharks kept away; the tour guide never ripped them off, not once—and yet they grumble now, complain of this and that, extortionary fees, bad airline java, hammerheads among the palms. They grab their mail and spin and go back home. Their flatscreens glow by night. Their cars, parked under trees, become unclean.

iv. Some people claim monopoly on strife

Oh, Agnes, with her too-bland face and terse delivery. The most she ever had to say was *Afternoon,* to me. Savaging those leaves as if they'd ever all be raked. Spritzing poison to protect her precious lawn. Pressing a palm on her lower back to show us all how hard she's laboured. On and on, sunrise, sunset, constant public toil. Mired in it like pelicans in tanker-sprung oil. And so she had a fire. Her fault, no doubt, her back turned to the stove. Barking through the mouthpiece at her daughter up in Illinois. Shrieking re a visit that was promised but repealed. When she turned back (as I imagine it), the deep fryer'd gone infernal, full-blown flame and rampant smoke and now the drywall, now the ceiling too, the insulation from those many years ago (her long-gone husband, Vern, had put it in), the attic trunks of letters and old toys. She ran outside, her voice a megaphone. And everybody cared. For once, they cared, they *rallied.* So of course I rallied too. And don't think I did not despise each generosity. Gave her food I'd saved up coupons just to buy at blowout prices. Gave her clothes I'd thought I might break out come early May. But not my figurines. She wouldn't want them anyway; she's got her phone, her litany of complaints.

v. A street of high old maples casting shade

A careless moment. I unstopped the drain in a basin I never use. There, cunningly, the angel shadows had amassed. As one, they rose. I'll tell you just one thing (and then I'll tell you one thing more). The shadow of an angel figurine, confined too long in pipes with cockroach eggs and meat grease, goes real bad. It soaks the very spirit of the pipe into itself. The second thing: the shadows lifted off, and braided each to each, and filled the room, and took a certain shape. At 7:30 my alarm goes off. I flail for SNOOZE. But in that second, with my dreaming dashed, such sentiments arise. You wouldn't care to know. I see my hand enacting deeds a crook would quail to see. Unneighbourly. And when the shadows filled my sight, they made—as best as I could tell—a perfect silhouette: the me who'd do the things I dream to do. I turned away. I squeezed my eyes right shut. And when I turned again, there were no shadows left. Unjudging sunlight filled the room; each item that it brushed was thus absolved. Floor by floor, my home resounded with a soothing choir. Just one unease remains: I haven't figured where the shadows went. I turn and turn, but all around is blazing bright. As if all shade has up and fled the world. The question is corrosion in my bones, a mastication on my stomach wall: where did they go? Throughout this home, where did the shadows go?

FROM **WISDOM OF THE ROCK, BOOK II**

There's very little wisdom in a rock.
Book I, I think, already covered this.
In short we're mostly dumb,

we chunks of stuff,
we hunkerers who don't dare stir
until some tosser frees us to the air.

I will admit: in flight,
once thrown, we fill with synapses
and find ourselves lit up with glutting thought.

What insights are bestowed! What intellection
roils! What coruscation we contain, until
we reach at last—and burst—the target eye.

SOMETIMES HYPOCHONDRIACS GET GENUINELY ILL

Trust me, I ought to know:
I'm one of them.
Or worry that I may be one.

A *World Book* from the Sally Ann
sprawls along my childhood shelf.
Volume A is faded—every night
I look up symptoms of appendicitis.

In the waste bin, cloaked
with soiled sheets and negatives
ripped in rage from cameras:
a shivering embryo.

I gaze upon a girl
who dances in a radiator,
white stuff pummelling her from above.

I know I'm kind of sick, but still I cook
a chop to perfect succulence. I clean
the countertops with rare intensity.
Something useless grows engorged in me.

LOT IN PERIL

Crust of tarmac; furrowed ruts
where many tires dug in; bright yellow lines
blurred and dulled with years but beautiful
in their antiquity; tar scars where winter cracks appeared
and so were plugged; great stout brown lamps,
four-bulbed, sky-conquering, weighted down
with concrete feet for ballast, bulbs expired,
some smashed by vandals with terrific aim
and handy rocks. My father as a tot would bike with friends
among these yellow lines, upon this rutted flesh. Once, cars
in copious fleets took refuge here—or *parked*,
the saying was—their blazing windows
visible for miles, noted by the circling birds
and even by the eyes in outer space;
full-on flocks of cars, diverse and large;
often too a van, an SUV,
or lumbering Winnebago, king of the lot.

Citizens, I've learned a grove of trees
threatens an incursion on this turf.
Roots busting up through concrete! Leaves blotting light!
Cones, needles, patterings of sap
littering the gnarled plain!
Soon animals will follow: birds
roosting in their heaps of broken twig;
rodents racing up the trunks and claiming nooks;
even foxes, deer, behemoth moose.
The lot we love's in peril. Things are dire.
I urge you to consider this: a lot gone wild
may never again restore itself. No car
can pass through clustered trunks.
Beyond the lot that lies beyond the lot,
the conifers have gathered and are chanting.

LETTER FROM A CREDITOR

Dear Mr. Norman:
We have not received the payment due November 1st.
Within three days, reply to this notice
or your service will be cut off.

We strongly advise you pay these funds
without delay. We're loath
to terminate the service.
Please don't make us do this.

We know there are circumstances.
We're sure you've had a painful day
and something roams behind your brow,
a lost fly trapped by a pane.

We can surmise the state of your surroundings.
Yes, we figure we can see you now,
slouched and weeping in the tattered chair
marked with stains from when you lost control.

It's clear you lost control.
Control took leave at a date unspecified
before November 1st. That much is plain;
the rest we've merely guessed.

Enclosed please find a sheaf of charts
delineating what you should have paid, and when.
This info will not help you, but the sheets ensure
a fanning-out of papers at your feet

as you sob and let them drop.
We hear the termites moving in your walls
and sense their hunger hollowing the planks
beneath your seat. Please pay the fees

outstanding. Insect bellies fill
with floor. Your chair will plunge
straight down and ever down. How far you'll fall,
we're sad to say, is way past our surmise.

A HAPPY DAY

Though the mailbox
nailed to my home's facade
ended up bereft of news;
though the barking of the dog
that keeps me up at night had morphed
into a keening human mewl;
and though the garbage can was tipped
and all my crumpled secrets tumbled out—

she smiled, gliding past. Her smile
was true, and told me she was glad
to smile at me. The big bike wheels
between her pedalling feet were fast and smooth.
Supple as a fish, the springtime sun
glimmered on the skin of every spoke.

SORRY IF YOU FEEL I MISSPOKE

Therefore should the statement be declined
or no I mean not down but maybe off as per
the wording best defined as *weaselly* or was it *like a snake*
post swallowing of weasel be respun
or in retraction made to spawn
a new reaction to an ancient pox?

I'm sorry that you didn't understand
if anyone offended if your sad beliefs
took offence at my former stated words
vis-à-vis the *weasel* comment and the *snake*
and other so-called slurs plus also too
know this: I meant no harm.

Don't crucify the messenger (that's me,
as per directives of analogy):
regrets are like opinions and/or snakes
no need to whinge, upset the cart of apples
grown to sweet fruition on a farm
where pitchforks really do mean harm.

Let's focus on core values going forward
emphasize the forward like the snake
has no reverse there was of course no real harm
just hypothetical I would regret that too.
The snake that eats fat prey is prone to choke.
I'm sorry if you feel I misspoke.

THE GRANTED WISH

For just one day, I was allowed to be my shaving cream.
What a way to get to know me!

Shocked awake by the influx of light
when my hand hauled open the mirror door,
exposing the medicine chest
where I was stored,

I saw five hairy fingers extend
and clutch my container,
crammed with pent-up force,
forbidden on planes for fear it could explode.

With a click the lid was pried off,
exposing a nozzle caked with dried cream.
My finger found a plastic nub and pressed
and out I surged, frothy extravagance.

My hands flattened me upon my facial skin.
Yet still I formed myself in whipped-up curds,
refusing to be dutiful, to spread out smooth.
How gleefully I vexed myself this way!

On my underside I could detect
the stubble poking up
into my subcutaneous cream-flesh,
stout bristles ready to be slain.

But then things took a turn.
Nothing about my wish included this,
nothing I'd read or heard had got me prepped:
the stubble screamed.

Its courage was illusory! It quailed at death.
Through fields of cream, the blade
whispered like a scythe to claim
a harvest howling with reluctance.

Then things got even worse:
although I was my shaving cream
and also was myself,
my stubble too, I learned, was part of me.

And so I felt the blade slide through the creamy me,
propelled by my own hand,
and yet I felt it slash the stubble-me,
bisecting me a dozenfold.

My many corpses snared
in clots of cream, I lay and bled.
And I bled too,
I mean the cheeks of me.

For in this foofaraw, my shaving hand
was made to tremble, and the razor slipped
and slipped again
and ribboned my poor neck.

And also then I saw my own cupped hands
rising, full of a pool—
the water that would be my death.
My cream-death, is what I mean.

The water loomed,
my face reflected, leering,
murderer and murdered
both at once, and leering so.

A fulsome splash, and the drowning began.
I dissipated, washed away,
and got to know the horrors of the drain
in my bathroom sink, a drain I'd never cleaned.

And as my clumps retreated down the pipe,
I issued another wish: that I be me,
shaver-me, blade-wielder-me,
and no one more.

I wobbled at the sink, returned to singular, my hands
planted for support on the fake marble counter,
their moisture causing them,
just a bit, to slide...

In the glass I regarded
the man I was, in his entirety
and separate from what he'd been before
(the shaving cream; the murdered hairs):

just me, a solid block, a single soul,
staring at his faint reflected self
made fainter by the steam
the slaughter—the hot water, more precisely—'d conjured up.

For my third wish, I asked for no more wishes.

SPELLING IN CONTEXT

There is no context for the spell.
Its incantations flee into a vacuum.
All the brew bewitches is the space
it occupies. The wand is non-

protruberant, for there is nothing
into which it might protrude.
And so the spell denotes its own damn form.
It primps before the glass and coos: *That's magic!*

We who tried to cast it
cower in the pockets of a hive
alive with silence, where the Queen's been plucked
by curators with macroscopic forceps.

Which way we turn
is predetermined by the turn
we have already taken. Spin and spin again
before the spit goes cool, the coals go ashen.

Hurlyburly's done for sure this time.
The woods are hobbled and they will not walk again.

GARDEN, AUTUMN, 6 P.M.

Effort's not enough
to tug the tired gut-sack
up the bucket wall
and so the slug,
sliding in its
fits-and-starts ascent,
must settle whether
this is climb
or plunge
and where
its rest will be.

Eyes rove
on undulating stalks.
The trail glistens.
Wind bothers beds
of weed and rush
and raindrops huddle
at the pail's base,
three of them, wobbly
and alert.

Everything sees,
or so it seems
to me, whose eyes
grow poorer
every minute.

Not long ago
I saw the slug ascend.
Now I cannot see
its gradual decline
and so can only guess
the slug is done

and bathes
in globes of rain
that now, this late,
this lost in shade,
withdraw themselves
from sight.

THE PERFECT OCTOPUS

The butcher had a waist-high fridge
heaped with seafood bound up tight
in plastic—severed bits or creatures
whole. Crab shells plucked of claws

with meat still cleaving. Shrimp,
legs primly tucked. And octopi
bundled into vacuum-sealed husks—
greenish-grey unwieldy clumps,

hideous but edible, I guess, and worth the price
jotted in Sharpie pen on cardboard squares.
Yet one was perfect, like a star
(more truly like a starfish), all its arms

curled out in symmetry, the suckers
evenly arrayed. What hand
or eye framed such exactitude?
I wouldn't know. But I know this:

precisely where the ink's discharged
or food pulled in or out or sex
asserts itself—a centred hole
nestled in the roots of arms—

the gap, I thought, resembled to the lash
a human eye by Botticelli.
It saw me watch. I almost heard it murmur:
Nothing evades perfection's gaze.

But really, in that rimy fridge,
huddled with others hauled from the sea,
crammed into plastic slathered with data
listing all its nutrients, awash

in self-preserving slime, this bundled beast
was tarted up to speak a cruder tongue.
The cephalopod said nothing noble.
Only *Eat me.*

FROM WISDOM OF THE ROCK, BOOK LXVIII

How did this dross extend
for sixty-seven books? What fluke
of rock effusion spurred me to produce

like stallions gone to stud? Give me a megaphone
that I can smash. A printing press
that I can butt to fragments. Give me dust.

Why did I start? I should have shut my yap
way back when the tectonic pressure
made me be. I should have suffered

silently, like trees beneath the axe.
But no, I spoke. Even the softest word,
set free, scoots off on frantic legs...

STUPID POEM

Deep down in my intestine, in my spleen or in my pith,
where spittle meets with bile and wrestles it
or cilia reach their eyeless fingertips
toward some bit of food to pilot it,
is an idea.

Or maybe just the semen of idea: the shrug
inside a cortex when the data riffles it
and makes it shift its atoms just a bit
or makes it feel some rough adhesive bug
is treading it.

But damn the intervening marmalade
spread ghastly like a membrane everywhere
to grip the thought that wriggles there
and fails to wrest itself away
from folds of grey.

You know I'm not as dumb as I appear.
Deep where sticky items co-adhere
a nub of substance lives—the rusted tip
embedded when the hunter chucked a spear.
You see where it has pierced me? Here—

RAILWAY EVENT

Each rail veers off course. They twist, like DNA,
then cross. The train inverts. A passenger
through same old glass regards new scenery
and marks a thud in the chest's right cavity.

Cows pausing by a bale regard
the Rorschach plume of smoke from the stack.
It looks no different than usual.
Breeze nibbles at the bale's extremities.

The noise—that steady chuffing respiration,
echo to the hurried horse
forced into gallop—sounds as it always did,
pistons just as ardent as before.

But clutching his punch, the conductor,
two days left until retirement,
traverses the disorient express,
his lifelong workplace flipped,

and wonders if he's heading forth or back
and if his wife, three stations off, still wears
a ring on her left hand, still loves him constantly
despite his constant forays far afield.

TO STAPLES

Staples, I can see you from my home.
Distinct against the dusk, your logo blazes.
Let me list the stuff I see from here:
you (Staples); the steeple of a church;
the naval docks; a grove of high-rise banks
(TD and RBC and Scotiabank);
a few hotels and other sundry sights
you might expect in a city of this size.

Staples, you have plied me with supplies
I may not need, or may, which help me work
and sometimes help me in my hobbies too.
You've given pens and printer cartridges
and paper by the sheaf. That sort of thing.
Your staff have been so helpful and so svelte.

NOTHING ARISES FROM THE SOUND

Don't be fooled by talk about the sound.

The water here's an inlet. Check a map.

But still we call it "the sound."

Across the water, in a bigger town, the folk say "inlet." A bridge connects us to them. With a toll.

The edge of the sound is dense with junk. Lobster traps and bicycles and shattered husks of hull.

Things go wrong. Systems fail at the sewage plant. Robots lose it in the factory. A boat is gashed and shit spills out.

At such times the water foams at its edge like the lips of a rabid dog.

At such times mudshark bellies huddle at the gravel shore.

One spring, the sound filled up with jellyfish. I mean, like, millions. The water turned half jelly. Not a cod could live.

Talk about the sound is mostly false.

People spew. They make stuff up.

Sometimes they'll tell you *everything arises from the sound.*

But look, I've seen the sound when shit goes south.

I've seen the bodies nosing up to shore.

I've seen the eyeballs plundered by the crabs.

Nothing—and trust me, please, I know—arises from the sound.

Nothing at all arises from the sound.

COLLISIONS

The cyclist and his bike were meshed
in the collision. I wonder
how the doctors disentangled them.
I'm certain that he got to hospital:
the driver of the car leapt out
and knelt beside him, and they spoke;
the cyclist and his bike were hoisted
straight into the car, and it was gone,
leaving tire prints and whispering witnesses.

Not long before, another car
had struck a boy I knew. The boy
went down. The car just fled.
The boy's brain never healed.
I think they caught the driver. I'm not sure.
It was a long investigation.

Since all of that, I have seen cars
plow into one another, knock down
lamps and signs. I've seen pedestrians
prone, motion walloped from their bodies.
But never again a driver emerge,
scoop up the victim as a lifeguard would
and gun it for the hospital;
nor a driver slam the gas and vanish,
leaving behind a child on the ground.

FREIGHT

At night the freight train murmurs to the floor.
The floor is moved and shudders in its boards
and we're awake. I wish I had a better ear.
A nail chatters in its slot, taps up against the wood
it split once, years ago. Its beat
might teach us of a nail's life: a single thrust,
baptismal, then the holding fast, the holding things
one to the other. This is a life that knows
with clarity its purpose—for a time. The ties
do loosen, though; and so the fretful nights
when train seduces floor, disordering the peace.
I wish I had a better ear. For all this fuss
the train sticks to its route: it perseveres,
moving and moving on and leaving things
a little more dislodged. And we're awake.

EVERYTHING HAS A REASON

but nothing conforms
to the reason it has.

Think of a baseball skinned
and nailed to a post
as a warning
to the unwelcome few.

Think of a leather belt.

You have knitted my mouth
at the lip. Your clacking needles
and goat-hair wool.
You promised a scarf.

I will sing with words half-formed.
My breath will be a torment in your ear.
I will eat through the tips of my fingers.

I HELPED THEM DRAW YOUR PICTURE AT THE STATION

We met just once, and it was brief.
Me in my serving apron. You with your gun
and fierce commands. And then you left.
There was a time I saw your face
in every crowd. That's not a compliment.
There was a time I smoked as if
to drain the city's dread, or spur on time,
which went so slow that night I'd swear I felt it

maybe stop. Or choke on its next second.
Let's face it: I have trouble coming out
with what I mean to say.
I stammer in the dark. The closing crew
extinguished all the lights. But I'm still trying.
Give me time. Come back tomorrow. Let me leave a note.

THE FLOOD

The band played schmaltz,
blared with its brass the swagger of "The Stripper,"
tried a tepid "All the Things You Are,"
drove me to the balcony to smoke.
And you were there already, smoking
in a black dress, and not four hours ago
the ring'd been slid onto your finger. New fiancée,
wriggling at the confines of a band
acquired too soon. And I, inhaling smoke and tar,
gaped that schmaltz would shunt me to such loveliness.

That's where the painted urn should freeze us,
just before your hand showed off its ornament
even as your eyes revealed a plea.
I sit now at a humble cubicle
and sort through stacks of other folks' mistakes
and wonder if I should have let that ring,
its meagre glister, bully me with mores.

The town where I work was flooded.
I sift through pages of reports
filed by those requiring recompense.
Digressions abound in the statements I read.
A basement window breaks, admitting the gush,
and a flotsam of story comes with it.
Why the pearls had sentimental value.
Where the parrot drowned had been acquired,
what phrases it preferred,
what flattery it lavished, what laments.

Undercarriages of cars corrode.
In one sedan two bodies bright with sweat
panted in unison. Something sharp was lodged
in a psyche. Let's commemorate the stifled cry

of ecstacy or brute regret, the handbrake
disengaged so the lever wouldn't jut.
When water came and the chassis
turned thirty degrees, the pair escaped.
Axles rust. Hubs are kissed by reeds.

In the lower quarters, houses were submerged
up to the eaves. One family on its roof played cards.
Played hard, ever intense about their poker.
The stakes were things below them, in the house,
warping and working loose in the water.
That was the joke: they gambled away the goods
fortune had already won from them.

The priest in the vestry quailed.
He had a thing about floods.
His wellingtons leaned in the corner, waiting.
He balked to put them on. See, floods:
God wiped the world clean with one, then swore
He'd finished with such smitings. No more torrents
grand enough to swallow up the earth.
Of course, a wealth of floods
since rampaged, swamping villages or worse,
and human history's a list of woes
that floods begat. (We're using *floods*
a little loosely here.) The priest perceived
a deluge as a border marker, staking out
what was and was not covered by the Covenant.
Every time a river sprang its banks,
its molecules were bounded by His Word
and when the damage broke all precedent,
our measure of what God meant
would have to shift. Revisions to the policy;
the coverage we thought we'd bought, denied.

The priest knelt on the vestry floor,
soaking his knees,
and prayed without articulation.
His empty boots felt water
creeping to their brims, but could not move,
and drank.

The flood was all those years ago.
All those. The ones that intervened,
regaling me with such quotidian cares
my face got grooved, my hair went stiff and white
and the keen light in faces when they saw me
dimmed. The town's recovered, though the dank
still dwells in things. The walls are dense with it.
And paperwork remains, the endless narrative
insisting it be heard. The endless totting up.

The force of sludge drawn to a sucking drain,
that urgent swirling down and in,
the thick-voiced slurp when air gets trapped
within the waning flow:
that force drew us, you and me; twined
our spiral threads. And then the contra-force:
past the drain you spin the other way,
go dissolute, the fluid scattering.
So the universe, they say, spreads itself
wider, thinner, greater, more diffuse.
When waters receded after the flood
into the river with a mighty gulp,
the old stream flowed
as it always had, but
thicker, muddied, snarled with all our lives.

Those who came here afterward
to cash in on cheapened real estate
never really dug the flood's extent.

Wrecked lots were scoured flat,
subjected to construction. One by one
the porches filled with barbecues and bikes
and lawn chairs folded anytime it rained.
Newcomers found their powers ailing here.
A softness in their joints, a squashy sloth.
Emerging from a troubled sleep,
they'd sense that something fluid caked their eyes
and everything they saw looked somehow warped.

Wherever you are now, whose eyes
put grappling hooks in my ribs, whose heat
infused me for the shortest stretch of time—
I trust you're not like these
latecomers to our town, their world
gone seepy, soft where sharp is best.
I hope your sky is a chorus of angles
and a corner turned is measured in degrees,
no slumping round a careworn curve.

Random bits of water life
transpire throughout the town:
seaweed garlanded to make a nest
for magpies; fishbones fossilized in curbs.
Once I found a starfish splayed beneath a bench.
Long dead, of course. Ants in a thin line
pilfered, piece by piece, a single arm.

A local gallery put on a show: *Reflections of the Deluge.*
Townsfolk were invited to submit. Most efforts
showed a heavy hand—biblical and such.
(The priest had done a gloomy one in oils.)
My favourite was a charcoal of an arm
snapped in a car wreck, with a shard of bone
thrust up through skin. I've no idea
what possible connection it could have

to our flood, any flood. I went to ask,
but a note on the desk read, *Gone for lunch.*

A boy who'd been hustled to safety
by his father's quick wits and jerry-rigged raft
(the father died; the raft was left intact)
acquired an appetite for all things dry.
It's obvious, I know;
so crude a path from grief. And yet he did.
Hoarded tindersticks and dolls
with cotton innards. Dreamed himself on plowed
and rutted earth, feet jammed deep in dirt,
arms wide to ward off crows;
sensed within his chest
rustlings of combustible straw.

I've got away from the point.
How that seems to happen, with the flood!
Seeping into every reminiscence.
The point is you—or us.
Smoke from our lips danced in the air,
strand interweaving strand, no hint of shame
or hesitation. It was perfect. That's my point.
In time, I'm sure, the strands were bound
to slither free. No lifelong cling for us.

Hand in hand, we swim above
a bed of wreckage. Gills pulse
at our throats.
You wear no ring.
Silt smears everything
but still we recognize the shapes; we point and coo.
We see upended chairs and knotted trikes;
dolls whose cloth bodies rotted off
leaving porcelain faces;
coils of rope unbraiding; kennels

whose denizens we hope escaped;
rusted flutes and gashed violins.

You point. The scales along your arm
catch light. You've spied a trunk
running over with its heap of clothes.
Emerging like the long black tongue
of someone just garrotted is your dress
from all those years ago. It shines with slime.
The loops and straps float free,
binding nothing, clutching only tide.

Something stirs the current, speeds it up. You turn
and so do I. Closing in behind us,
vast as the hand that drowned our town:
a fish. Face pestilent with growths—
limp shiitake strands and cauliflower cysts.

You know what's in that belly, that esophagus,
what coats the rows of teeth. And so do I. It leaks
like squid's ink into water, which is everywhere.
All we do's in water. All we secrete.
Within the fish is born the simple shape
we made as children, moulding children's clay,
and then forgot. The ink flows free
and threatens to engulf us both.
I turn to you—last chance—move in to kiss.

But where your face was, nothing's left.
The silt, the reeds, the shifting minnow schools
obliterate your form. No guiding light appears;
the only stars are fish, and they're no help.
They're busy growing back their stolen arms.

NOTES

Each stanza of "The Answers" is an excerpt from a different on-the-record interview formerly stored on the author's digital recorder.

The technique of replacing the expected word with a homonym (or something close to it), as deployed in "School Day," is borrowed from Linda Besner's "P-S-E-U-D-O-H-O-M-O-P-H-O-N-E."

Each line of "The Turnips" incorporates the anagram of "turnips" from the corresponding line of bpNichol's "Historical Implications of Turnips."

Each line of "Dr. F Attends a Show" ends with the same word as the corresponding line of Margaret Atwood's "Speeches for Doctor Frankenstein."

The imagery in the fourth stanza of "Sometimes Hypochondriacs Get Genuinely Ill" is inspired by a scene in David Lynch's *Eraserhead.*

"Stupid Poem" responds to an April 1, 2011, post on Stuart Ross's *Bloggamooga* blog, which read, in part, "A person said it's National Poetry Month. I said ... write some stupid poem and title it 'Stupid Poem.'"

ACKNOWLEDGEMENTS

Versions of poems in this book first appeared in *Arc Poetry Magazine, Contemporary Verse 2, Literary Review of Canada, Ottawater, Peter F. Yacht Club, The Rusty Toque, Taddle Creek, The Week Shall Inherit The Verse* and *THIS Magazine*. "Up Near Wawa" was awarded the 2008 Confederation Poets Prize, judged by Joan Crate.

Huge thanks to Stuart Ross, a brilliant and invaluable editor, and Denis De Klerck, who makes it all happen. Also to the many people who have helped my poems along with feedback, encouragement and venues in which to write and read; for this batch, particular thanks to Dani Couture, Lee Henderson (for pointing out the beauty of the word *Nokia*), Max Middle, Kathryn Mockler, Lillian Necakov, Conan Tobias and—as ever, for everything—Melanie Little.

Peter Norman was born in Vancouver, and has since lived in Victoria, Ottawa, Calgary, Halifax, Dartmouth and now Toronto, where he works as a freelance editor. His first poetry collection, *At the Gates of the Theme Park* (Mansfield Press, 2010), was a finalist for the Trillium Poetry Book Award.

OTHER BOOKS FROM MANSFIELD PRESS

POETRY

Leanne Averbach, *Fever*
Nelson Ball, *In This Thin Rain*
George Bowering, *Teeth*
Stephen Brockwell & Stuart Ross, eds., *Rogue Stimulus: The Stephen Harper Holiday Anthology for a Prorogued Parliament*
Diana Fitzgerald Bryden, *Learning Russian*
Alice Burdick, *Flutter*
Alice Burdick, *Holler*
Margaret Christakos, *wipe.under.a.love*
Pino Coluccio, *First Comes Love*
Gary Michael Dault, *The Milk of Birds*
Pier Giorgio Di Cicco, *The Dark Time of Angels*
Pier Giorgio Di Cicco, *Dead Men of the Fifties*
Pier Giorgio Di Cicco, *The Honeymoon Wilderness*
Pier Giorgio Di Cicco, *Living in Paradise*
Pier Giorgio Di Cicco, *Early Works*
Pier Giorgio Di Cicco, *The Visible World*
Salvatore Difalco, *What Happens at Canals*
Christopher Doda, *Aesthetics Lesson*
Christopher Doda, *Among Ruins*
Rishma Dunlop, *The Body of My Garden*
Rishma Dunlop, *Lover Through Departure: New and Selected Poems*
Rishma Dunlop, *Metropolis*
Rishma Dunlop & Priscila Uppal, eds., *Red Silk: An Anthology of South Asian Women Poets*
Ollivier Dyens, *The Profane Earth*
Jaime Forsythe, *Sympathy Loophole*
Carole Glasser Langille, *Late in a Slow Time*
Suzanne Hancock, *Another Name for Bridge*
Jason Heroux, *Emergency Hallelujah*
Jason Heroux, *Memoirs of an Alias*
Jason Heroux, *Natural Capital*
John B. Lee, *In the Terrible Weather of Guns*
Jeanette Lynes, *The Aging Cheerleader's Alphabet*
David W. McFadden, *Be Calm, Honey*
David W. McFadden, *What's the Score?*
Leigh Nash, *Goodbye, Ukulele*
Lillian Necakov, *The Bone Broker*
Lillian Necakov, *Hooligans*
Peter Norman, *At the Gates of the Theme Park*
Natasha Nuhanovic, *Stray Dog Embassy*
Catherine Owen & Joe Rosenblatt, with Karen Moe, *Dog*
Corrado Paina, *The Alphabet of the Traveler*
Corrado Paina, *The Dowry of Education*
Corrado Paina, *Hoarse Legend*
Corrado Paina, *Souls in Plain Clothes*
Matt Santateresa. *A Beggar's Loom*
Matt Santateresa, *Icarus Redux*
Ann Shin, *The Last Thing Standing*
Jim Smith, *Back Off, Assassin! New and Selected Poems*
Jim Smith, *Happy Birthday, Nicanor Parra*
Robert Earl Stewart, *Campfire Radio Rhapsody*
Robert Earl Stewart, *Something Burned on the Southern Border*
Carey Toane, *The Crystal Palace*
Priscila Uppal, *Summer Sport: Poems*
Priscila Uppal, *Winter Sport: Poems*
Steve Venright, *Floors of Enduring Beauty*
Brian Wickers, *Stations of the Lost*

FICTION

Marianne Apostolides, *The Lucky Child*
Sarah Dearing, *The Art of Sufficient Conclusions*
Denis De Klerck, ed., *Particle & Wave: A Mansfield Omnibus of Electro-Magnetic Fiction*
Paula Eisenstein, *Flip Turn*
Marko Sijan, *Mongrel*
Tom Walmsley, *Dog Eat Rat*

NON-FICTION

George Bowering, *How I Wrote Certain of My Books*
Denis De Klerck & Corrado Paina, eds., *College Street–Little Italy: Toronto's Renaissance Strip*
Pier Giorgio Di Cicco, *Municipal Mind: Manifestos for the Creative City*
Amy Lavender Harris, *Imagining Toronto*
David W. McFadden, *Mother Died Last Summer*

To order Mansfield Press titles online, please visit mansfieldpress.net